You Can
Your Own ~~Book~~

CW00968251

by Paul Johnson

Contents

LONGMAN

Concertina books

Concertina books are probably the oldest kind of book. They were first made in China. They are very simple books made from single sheets of paper. The paper is folded in a special way.

A long time ago in Africa, a baby whale named Susie, who lived in a swimming pool heard 'Meeow.' Susie looked up

2

and saw a big black cat. "Hello" said Susie. "Why are you panting?" "Because I'm being chased by a fox." Said the cat.

3

"I know." shouted Susie, "Jump on my back. Now I will repay you for your kindness." said the cat. "I wish I was in the sea."

4

Said Susie. The cat produced a box of big balloons, blew them up and tied them on to Susie's body.

5

How to make a concertina book

 Lay a piece of A4 or A3 paper in front of you with the longest side facing you.

 Fold the paper vertically in half.

 Fold it horizontally in half.

Open the paper so that it has only one vertical fold.

Fold it vertically in half again.

Open up the whole sheet of paper. You will have eight rectangles on the paper.

 Fold the sheet horizontally in half.

 Fold in half vertically along the middle creased line.

 Fold the outside pieces of paper back on themselves. (You should now have a zig-zag shape.)

Numbering the pages

Hold the book like this.

Start to number the book from the inside folds. Start with number 2 on the page furthest to the left. Number the pages up to 5.
Turn the book over and from the left number 6, 7, 8 and then 1. Number 1 is the front cover.

The design of the pages

Your book will look more professional if you leave a margin around your writing and drawing. So cut out a card template in the shape of a rectangle 1cm smaller than your page if using A4 paper, and 2cm smaller if using A3 paper.

Place the template on the middle of each page and then draw a faint line carefully around it. Do not write or draw outside this line in the margin.

Origami books

You have probably seen animals made out of folded paper. This way of folding paper is called origami, and it comes from Japan. There are many kinds of origami books and some of them are very difficult to make. But this one is the simplest of them all.

An origami book

How to make an origami book

Turn back to page 3 and follow the instructions numbered 1–6. You should now have a sheet of paper in front of you that looks like this:

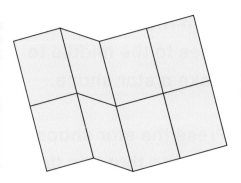

Fold the paper vertically in half.

Cut through the middle panels on the folded edge.

Open up the whole sheet of paper.

Fold the paper horizontally in half.

Hold the left and right sides of the paper. Push the left and right sides to the middle to make a star shape.

Press the star shape down so that it is flat.

Fold the pages each side of the fold on top of each other to make the origami book.

Presenting your ideas

In illustrated story books, the words and pictures are usually arranged differently on each page. If you decide to start a page with writing and then have an illustration in the space underneath, you could put this arrangement the other way round on the next page. It will make your page spreads much more exciting to look at.

Different page designs

Books with pop-ups

One of the most unusual things you can do with a book is to make pop-ups inside it. A pop-up is made from a piece of folded paper inside a page. When you open the page, the pop-up springs upright.

Some pop-ups can be very difficult to make, but this one can be made easily, just using a pair of scissors.

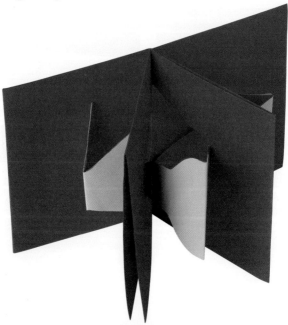

How to make a book with pop-ups

Follow the instructions 1–3 for the origami book on page 7. Then continue as follows:

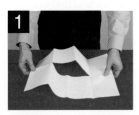

Open up the whole sheet of paper.

Fold over the left side to the centre.

Then fold the right side to the centre.

Cut through the bottom left fold as shown. Don't cut more than half-way across the page.

Then cut higher up the bottom left fold as shown. Don't cut more than half-way across the page.

Repeat for the right-hand side fold as shown.

Crease all the shapes you have cut.

Press back flat again all the shapes you have just creased.

Open up the whole sheet.

Fold down the origami book again, using the instructions on page 8.

When you fold the cut pages, make sure that the cuts are all on the inside of the book.

Now, one by one, lift out the middle parts of the cut pages to make the pop-ups.

Preparing to write and draw

As the pop-ups are in the middle of the pages, plan to put your writing above or below the middle of the page. Always try to make your handwriting as attractive to look at as your artwork.

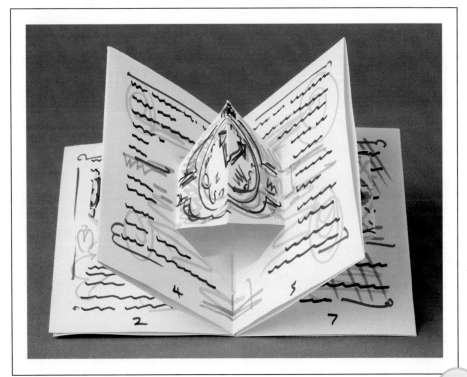

Books with removable objects

With most books you just read them and look at the pictures. But some books have things that you can take out of them, like letters and games.

We all like nice surprises. We love opening envelopes, especially if we think there is something exciting inside.

How to make a book with removable objects

Crease a sheet of A3 paper vertically and horizontally. Open it out.

Using scissors, cut through one horizontal crease.

Fold the paper down (from top to bottom).

You will have two loose panels. Fold one backwards and the other forwards. This makes a four-page book.

To make the pocket, open up the whole sheet. Using a pencil and ruler, draw two vertical lines through the centre of the top right panel. Leave a space at the top and bottom of the panel.

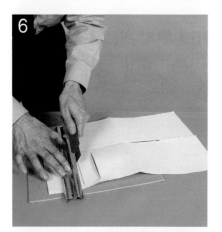

Now cut through the lines with a craft knife and steel ruler.

Always use a cutting board when using a craft knife. Keep your fingers away from the knife blade.

Fold the sheet as you did before. The book now has a pocket for an invitation or letter.

Making an origami envelope

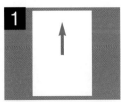 Lay a sheet of A4 paper in front of you with the shortest side facing you.

 Pull the paper over to find the middle of it and put a mark there. But do not fold the paper.

 Fold the top corners of the paper in to the middle, so that they make a point.

Fold the sheet of paper in half horizontally.

Turn the paper over so that the point is underneath.

Fold one side to the middle.

Fold the other side to the middle.

Fold the top rectangle down as far as it will go.

Place your fingers under the rectangle and open the folds beneath it. Tuck the rectangle inside those folds.

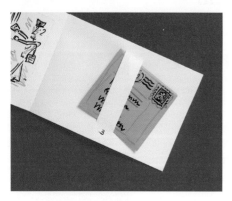

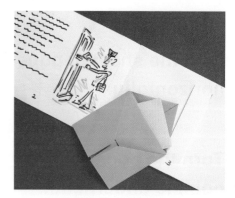

A letter in an origami envelope

Wallet books

The pages of a wallet book open like compartments, and they hold the kind of things that you would expect to find in a real wallet – money, plastic cards, letters, photographs and bus tickets. If you write a story which includes lots of things like this, try presenting your story as a wallet book.

How to make a wallet book

Follow instructions 1–6 for the concertina book on page 3. You should now have a sheet of paper that looks like this:

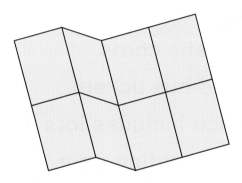

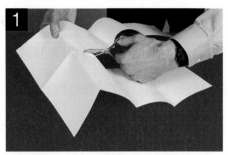

Using scissors, cut through the centre first three panels.

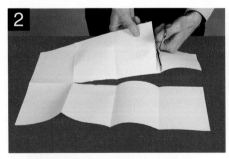

Using scissors, cut away the bottom left side panel.

Cut away a small part of the next panel. This will make a tuck-in flap.

Take a craft knife, and carefully cut three slots as shown.

Drop the top four panels over the bottom three.

Concertina the top panels so that they lie on the bottom panel as shown.

Fold the first page with the tuck-in flap over all the other pages and tuck in the slot on the back of the wallet.

What to write about

You have four pages on which to write and illustrate a story about the wallet. Do its contents give your readers clues about whom it belongs to? Is there a secret message in the wallet? Does your story tell us about it, how it got there, and what it means?

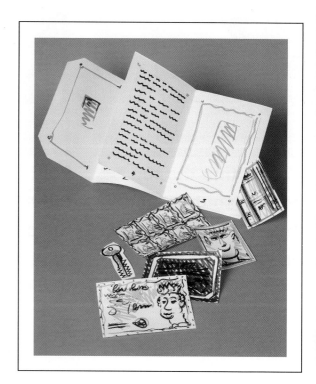

The wallet book with its contents removed

Glossary

A4 the size of a piece of paper – 297 mm × 210 mm

A3 the size of a piece of paper – 297 mm × 420 mm

artwork hand-drawn illustrations in a book

compartment a place which is separated from another place

horizontal goes from left to right (opposite of vertical)

margin space around the edge of the page where there is no writing or drawings

origami a special way of folding paper. The first people to use origami were from Japan

spread what you see when a book lies open – the left and right pages facing each other

template a flat shape used to draw around to produce a ready-made border

vertical goes from top to bottom (opposite of horizontal)

Further information

Other books by Paul Johnson

A Book of One's Own, Hodder and Stoughton
Pop-up Paper Engineering, Falmer
Literacy Through the Book Arts, Hodder and Stoughton
Books Searching for Authors, Hodder and Stoughton

Museums which have book exhibitions

The British Museum, Great Russell Street, London WC1B 3DG

The Victoria and Albert Museum, Cromwell Road, South Kensington, London SW7 2RL

The Bethnal Green Museum of Childhood, Cambridge Heath Road, London E2 9PA